Operations in the Time of Industry 4.0

A guide to managing the clash of digitalization and real life operations

By Stefan Tontsch

AF199773

Operations in the Time of Industry 4.0

Stefan Tontsch

Impressum

Bibliografische Information der Deutschen Nationalbibliothek:
Die Deutsche Nationalbibliothek verzeichnet diese Publikation
in der Deutschen Nationalbibliografie; detaillierte
bibliografische Daten sind im Internet über http://dnb.dnb.de
abrufbar.

Lektorat: PaperTrue
Korrektorat: Kurt Jansen
Illustrated by: Francesca Rose - DesignSlang
Nachwort: Daniel Krauss

Herstellung und Verlag: BoD – Books on Demand,
Norderstedt

ISBN: 978-3-7481-0981-5

CONTENTS

INTRODUCTION

We all know about the stereotypical tech company: highly educated young people entering futuristic high-rises in Silicon Valley, performing magic that ends up in creating a powerful new product or something on your smartphone.

However, there also exists a workforce which is engaged in hitting nails with hammers, ringing doorbells, carrying parcels up stairs, driving trains, and mowing the lawns in the city parks. The majority of these people are neither in their twenties nor are they multi-lingual computer science graduates.

The contrast between these two worlds is stark and very real. Most tech businesses work on a shared economy approach, allowing them to avoid solving the challenges of other working realities, as tackling these would impede their rapid growth. Uber, for example, isn't inclined to worry about the oil change procedures of the taxis operating under its purview, or decide on the best choice of wind-shield wiper.

If they were to take care of it, the number of drivers and cars they could integrate would be significantly reduced, because the level of effort would drastically increase.

The list of tech businesses avoiding real, hands-on operations is long, for obvious reasons. Of course, when I talk about operations, I mean the maintenance of on-site infrastructure as well as actual customer contact.

The process of improving the professional processes of a hotel, for example, could take months if not years of training until every housekeeper is able to clean a room with consistent speed and quality, and until every food services worker is able to ensure the timely availability of the appropriate amount of coffee for the breakfast buffet.

On the other hand, for the optimization of a taxi service, local experience is required to be aware of which garage delivers the price and quality balance needed to run the business successfully. This can't be ignored, as outsourcing entails a separate cost.

Increasing the turnover of your company by a factor of 10 in two years isn't possible under these realities, and the time and investment required to build a physical hotel is greater still.

At first, these examples might appear irreconcilable, and it may seem that the world of work will increasingly be divided into a small group of digital sorcerers—organizing the platforms and taking the greater share of the margins—and a large group of muggles taking care of the grunt work.

Looking at big corporations, this is something that has already happened. Where are the young, dynamic, and well-educated workers with the highest potential? They are in the marketing, sales, business development, and IT divisions. They are not found in operations. As a result of this situation, most operations workforces in industrialized countries are ageing dramatically, thereby activating a feedback cycle in which operations becomes even less attractive for digital people.

People with a digital mindset fully understand the opportunities brought about by automation in the form of artificial intelligence (AI) and big data. These people will not choose a career based on optimizing the cleaning speed of a housekeeper.

Another example is found in rail companies. Until the 70's, being a train driver was considered a leadership position. Boys dreamt of being one, application lists were long, and access was difficult. In contrast, the sales department was just a necessary overhead required for selling paper tickets at stations—useful but almost meaningless when compared to a driver. This has changed dramatically.

Today, the game is won by the sales team by activating demand, placing the right ads in search engines, optimizing prices in extensive yield tools, and managing to turn casual users into heavy users with the help of smart incentive systems. Train drivers? Yeah, we need them too...

The profession of flight attendants has seen one of the most dramatic drops in job prestige, since the time when they were still called stewards and stewardesses.

Right into the early 90's, this was a dream profession. I watched an interview with a retired Air France executive who was working in the 70's, who stated that only a very small share of young women was selected from the army of applicants, and they were considered so perfect that, on average, they were married after 7 months by the wealthy customers. As this was the 70's, they often quit their jobs soon after.

An interesting side note is that it was not only desirable for the young women to become stewardesses but also for the wealthy clients to marry one. Wages and influence in the company were connected to that status. I know a Lufthansa stewardess who, living alone, managed to buy a 3-bedroom apartment in downtown Frankfurt in the late 90's.

Compare that situation with today. Would a father advise his daughter to take up a career as a flight attendant at a low-cost airline? Pay is barely above minimum wage, and the only people still entering this industry are working migrants from countries which pay even less. Buying a 3-bedroom apartment in downtown Frankfurt? Impossible!

So, is operations doomed to a future of being a meaningless sidekick to the digital world?

The exact opposite is true. In a digital world, the only companies that have a future are those that manage to digitalize their operations.
However, in order to leverage digital solutions in operational processes, we need to change our ways—quickly and dramatically.

This book holds some good advice on how to do it.

If you assume for a second that your digital transition has already taken place, consider how do digital and operations go hand in hand? The answer is: surprisingly well! Surprising, because this is so rarely applied.

What makes perfect operations? It is usually about:

Repeatedly and quickly delivering identical and flawless quality, anytime

And if that sounds too theoretical, let's take a simple example. What is perfect operations in an ice cream store? It's an employee who scoops precisely the same-sized ice cream ball into a cone in a fast and friendly manner. They never make a mistake with regard to providing the correct amount of change, respect all hygiene protocols, and are available at the times at which people desire ice cream and also at short notice, such as if there is an unexpected heat-wave.

But if you consider the following qualities:

- Repeat
- Quick
- Identical
- Flawless
- Anytime

You are, in effect, not talking about the qualities of humans but the qualities of machines.

Stop trying to turn your employees into robots

The list of efforts put into attempting to make employees as robotic as possible is endless.

- Training repetitive work (repetitively)—like my poor university friend, who was put next to a scale for half a day to learn how to scoop the exact right weight into one ice cream ball

- Mystery shopper programs

- Surveillance systems and automated KPIs on individuals—like 'seconds per clean hotel room'

- Incentive systems to achieve perfection

- Legal tricks to evade working time regulations

- Plus many, many more...

Apart from the fact that it is silly to try to make people behave like robots, it fosters the wrong culture and leads to the previously-described loss in prestige. If you optimize everything toward complete compliance with processes, there are two devastating results: people stop thinking about what they do (why should they not?), and the only possible deviation is failing in achieving perfection.

The latter leads to a loss of prestige because operations is only a subject in management if it fails. Operations such as this can never result in positive news: either the ice cream ball is perfect (no issue) or it is wrong (issue).

Upon seeing the monotony of the work, the outsider perceives operations as a group of morons screwing up every now and then. This is not a place which anyone with a choice would want to work in.

Foster the unique abilities of humans to organize how machines could take over this part.
As there is a big lag of digitalization in operations in general, there is no other area in which fruits are hanging so low.

Let's start turning your operations into digital operations. Enjoy the read.

BUSINESS POTENTIAL OF OPERATIONS 4.0

It doesn't take long to figure the difference in company value between a tech company and an old economy business: It is in the multiple of the turnover.

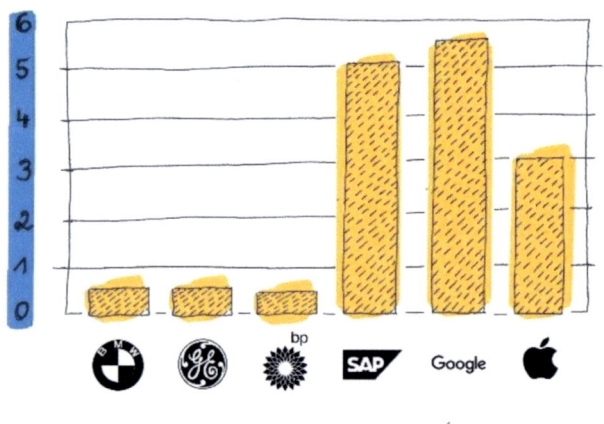

🟨 MARKET CAPITALISATION / TURNOVER

You can think whatever you like about the true value of a tech company, but it is a fact that, on the same turnover, their value is 6 to 12 times higher.

Without drilling too deep into the reasons (as it would lead us off topic), the fundamental investor expectation behind it is that the market sees a more promising future for tech companies than for old economy companies.

On a tech platform you can scale, grow, and enter new markets with very little effort. You can adapt to changes quickly, and you avail of opportunities for great margins when scaling.

One the other hand, old economies are stuck in their ways and are often unable to move swiftly enough. Any disruption in their industry has the potential to blow them away.

Disruption will happen. Be the driver, not the victim

There are plenty of old examples of this. Mail order houses, which disappeared from the market to be replaced by online shopping in just a few years. Encyclopedia editors with a history of hundreds of years, swept away by Wikipedia.

There are recent examples too, like classic banks losing ground to FinTechs. A milestone pertaining to this phenomenon was observed in 2018, when the 2nd largest German bank had to leave the German stock index (DAX) to be replaced by the FinTech Wirecard.

Other disruptions are also becoming visible. For instance, the brands you find for electric cars are not the classic car manufacturers anymore. It's quite likely that the market for electric vehicles will look very different to the one for combustion cars.

Turning your business digital has, therefore, two important upsides. It dramatically increases your company value, and it will prepare it for future disruptions. The effort needed for the transition is tiny by comparison.

17

Overcoming Classical Trade-Offs

One of the reasons why old economy businesses cannot improve, change, or grow quickly is that they usually face decisions that incur quite a lot of expenses if they want to do so.

The higher the price for a necessary step, the more one tends to avoid it. The digital transition, however, would aid you in lowering the cost for change, thereby ensuring your business becomes agile again.

Break: good service = expensive service

Consider the sphere of customer service. The classical trade-off is that the more services you want to offer, the more people you need to hire in order to deliver them. However, if you manage to resolve customer queries by way of terminals, bots, self-service solutions and automated processes, you would be able to:

- Provide better services in every language, round the clock, and with 100% accuracy

  Simultaneously, you would be able to:

- Save resources, as the system can scale up without incurring additional costs

Break: update of product = high investment

The same applies to new product generations; instead of having to invest heavily in hardware improvement, you could employ simple ways to upgrade. There will be more details provided on this in the following chapter on hardware legacies.

Break: rollout everywhere = many employees everywhere

Old economy businesses mostly produce a large share of the product offered in-house. Therefore, growth opportunities outside their home market involve high investment in terms of bringing in the necessary production infrastructure, including hiring a competent workforce. This necessitates complications and therefore becomes time consuming. Finally, it negatively impacts the decision to perform the action in the first place.

It is much easier to provide an operational platform solution that is applicable everywhere than to export your infrastructure to other locations.

No More Maintenance of Old Systems

To conclude this chapter on business opportunities, you need to take a look at the effort you have to make to maintain old hardware, software, and procedures. Most companies are full of these, and it is usually not at all easy to see how much money it costs to keep up with them.

This problem consists of two aspects. The first is how much you actually spend extra, compared to a state-of-the-art system. The second (often much more critical) aspect comprises the business opportunities you miss by being stuck with them.

How much do your legacies cost you?

Try this short exercise. Make a list of the following:

- jobs you don't need when getting rid of legacies
- compromises you wouldn't have made last year, if it wasn't for the status quo
- workplaces that would not be necessary if it wasn't for a legacy system

Take this as a starting point for a rough estimate of how much money you are talking about. If the assessment is honest, it is usually massive. The only thing keeping you from changing it is the transition.

However, this must never be the reason. Let's start with these legacies.

KILL YOUR LEGACIES

One fundamental difference between digital and analog businesses is their speed of development. If you aim to adapt your operations to the speed of digital, you need to get rid of all the things which hinder you from being fast. And the word that best describes these things is 'legacy'.

Before you can even start to turn your business digital, you need to get yourself room to move. As a matter of fact, operations has usually entangled itself in a thorny hedge of legacy vines, leaving it stuck and vulnerable to any intruder disrupting your industry.

The first important step in the process of turning old-school operations digital is therefore to thoroughly list all the legacies you can find in your company. Obviously, you can't get rid of all of them at once, but this chapter offers a strategy for starting, and on what you should focus.

What exactly to look for in a legacy?

If you had to choose between replacing your present process, system, or tool with a brand new art, would you still keep yours? If the answer is no, it's a legacy

This exercise requires a longer reflection period, as we are all inclined to oversee things we have gotten used to in our close environment. But those are exactly the potential areas for legacies in your system, because they have been around forever.

Do not continue until you have this step right, because you might still find yourself tied up in too many vines to be able to start moving quickly.

In general, we find three areas of legacies:

- Hardware legacies
- IT legacies
- (Legal) regulations

You can use these categories as a guide for identifying yours.

You should also consider applying out-of-the-box approaches to finding them—invite outsiders to brainstorm with you, ask children, envision the removal of a certain process and follow the chain of what could go wrong. You could even recall past big operational challenges (a storm, a blackout, and so on)—regardless of whether they were mastered or turned out to be a disaster. What and who was involved, and why? What was the role and use? What helped, what inhibited you?

If you found none, or only a few legacies, the chances are that you didn't leave your box.

In order to give you an idea of what you should be looking for, I added a number of examples from different industries to give you a better idea.

Stick to processes, tools and systems; don't complain about colleagues

There is a reason I didn't list stubborn, backward-looking

colleagues as an area of legacy, even though they can be a relevant, hindering factor. This is because you have to get your system right before addressing the question of who is the right fit. There is an entire chapter later focusing on the implications for your workforce. However, it is a result of the transition and not the starting point.

Hardware Legacy

What is a Hardware Legacy and what isn't, even if it's old

On a very generic level, things we use have different life spans and innovation cycles. A short lifespan allows for a quick innovation speed. The downside is the cost of replacing the old product. In a purely digital environment, the cost of replacing a product becomes small or even negligible, for instance, updating software.

The picture changes dramatically when big machinery is involved. This is often due to the simple fact that it is complicated to develop and produce it. In addition, the machinery needs to prove its stability and safety, which involves tests and homologation cycles, all of which take time. In some cases, even deploying the machinery after it is developed and built is an expensive affair.

Think of a ski-lift as an example. Upgrading an old drag-lift to a state-of-the-art chairlift is an expensive decision that needs to pay off over many years.

A 20-year old drag-lift is a hardware legacy

However, not everything that is old is automatically a legacy. A very simple example is a scaffold. The fundamental principle hasn't changed for millennia.

A 20-year old scaffold system is no hardware legacy

This is because there is no updated system at present that is significantly superior.

Hardware with a lifespan of around 5–20 years is often not that critical—only very few things that have an average age of 10 years are ridiculously outdated. Think of a delivery truck of a logistics company. Take as a rule of thumb the following:

Things you replace after 10 years are not your problem

The situation is totally different for items that are meant to be used for 20–50 years. If your product is outdated soon after deploying it, you will have to go a long way to keep up with it.

A good example for this is the introduction of the first high speed trains (ICE) in Germany in 1991, based on a prototype from 1985. However, between 1985 and 1991 laptops experienced their breakthrough and became very popular in the late 80's and early 90's. The same applies to mobile phones.

For both products, there was a significant demand for sockets on trains, but that ship had sailed as the 1985 setup –without sockets– was applied and this missing feature became a painful shortfall of the ICE model for over a decade. This is not to speak of the terrible phone reception on a train, as it was never designed for such a thing.

Then, between 2005 and 2008, the first-generation ICE trains underwent a long and expensive refurbishment program, updating much more than just the sockets. Eventually, there were sockets everywhere, as well as

25

mobile phone signal repeaters in the coaches. Unfortunately, in 2007, the smartphone was invented, and soon there was a great demand for WiFi on trains. Once again, the trains had a significant shortfall immediately after delivery. This time, it took 8 years to fix the aforementioned issue in another big retrofit program.

So, we can derive two lessons from this:

Just before introducing things you plan to use for 20–50 years, double check if they are not going to be outdated upon roll-out

It was possible to fix the shortfall and still use the thing. 28 years have now passed, and they are still running

If 50 years seem long, there is a significant amount of hardware that is used for even longer—and I am not talking about vintage, nostalgia, or museum hardware.

In particular, infrastructure can often have a longer lifespan, of 70, 100 or more years.

Think about the Hoover Dam—active since 1931. After 50 years, the turbines were exchanged for modern ones, nearly doubling the output. Or the Suez Canal—opened in 1869 (!). Only after more than a century, between 2009 and 2015, was a fundamental reconstruction carried out to increase the capacity. These examples show that:

Even hardware over 50 years old can be updated and useful

If you look at the examples mentioned above, you will find two types of hardware legacies—Customer Facing and Efficiency Focused.

Compare, for instance, the example of the ski-lift with the new turbines in the Hoover Dam.
Having a chairlift rather than a drag-lift significantly changes the customer experience. But this will be even more so if it becomes a market standard (as it actually did), and in this case there is a risk of customers ignoring your ski-resort.

Customer-Facing hardware legacies have downside potential that can suddenly materialize

The refurbishment of a turbine is an entirely different case. The electricity produced retains its value, even if it is produced inefficiently by outdated turbines. If you consider revamping the turbines, there is no time pressure; it is a simple case of business. If you earn more with a higher output that offsets the cost of the new turbines, then it is a good deal and you do it. If not, you don't, and life goes on— unlike the draglift example.

Efficiency-Focused legacies are a business case, with no time pressure

Of course, life is not black and white. Many hardware legacies will be somewhere between those extremes. Take, for example, the Suez Canal. It is, in principal, more on the Efficiency-Focused side, but given that the missing capacity had already caused shipping companies to implement alternative routes for vessels too big to pass through the canal, it had a Customer-Focused aspect too.

If you look at the difference in the magnitude of the effect, you need to keep in mind that you must

Be much more alert about potential Customer-Facing legacies

than you would be about Efficiency-Focused ones.
This has two implications:

1. You need to double-check if the Customer Facing part of your product is still up to date just before the very last point of no return.

2. You need to allow flexibility in the design.

These were the two fundamental mistakes which Deutsche Bahn made when introducing the ICE. It was already apparent in the late 80's that laptops and mobile phones would be the next big thing. Ignoring that in 1991 was an avoidable mistake. Unfortunately, the structural technical components and the customer-facing interior of the train were too closely connected, technically. Resolving the Customer-Facing problem (introducing sockets) without touching the whole system was therefore impossible.

Between 2005 and 2008, the first mistake was repeated – the necessity for WiFi was already apparent, yet ignored. However, this time there was technical flexibility for the retrofitting of WiFi in trains, thereby reducing the reaction time to half of that of the first example.

At this point, many operations managers tell me that this is impossible to do, because things are so old and complicated in their particular case, trends are unclear, their distinct situation very individual, and so on.
My advice here is usually to make an analogy. If the pain of outdated Customer-Facing hardware becomes personal, you become much more creative and much less tolerant of shortfalls.

Imagine you inherit a little house from the 1930's. Would you tolerate having a toilet in the yard, no phone, no Internet, and no fridge? Of course not. You would find ways to preserve the fundamentally healthy structure of the house while introducing water pipes, wires, and a state-of-the-art kitchen, regardless of how complicated this would be. As this would be on your personal budget, you would certainly find financially feasible ways to do it.

Take the Customer-Facing hardware legacies personally

and you'll have started your own journey into the transition to digital operations.

To conclude the ICE story, the WiFi issue was solved within a year after the owner publicly announced that the CEO's contract would only be prolonged if WiFi were introduced— that proved personal enough!

After you have successfully identified all the hardware legacies in your business, you should arrange them according to the following scheme:

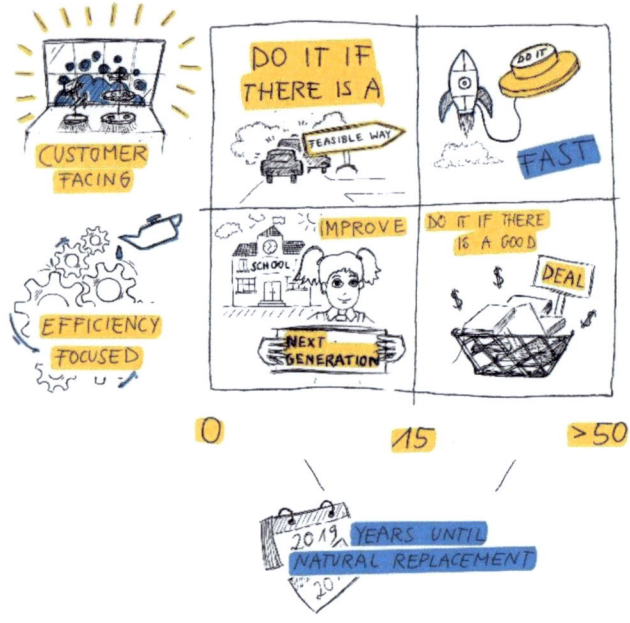

The ones which keep you from moving quickly are found in the

top right corner—they are critical

in the sense that they can kill your business suddenly if

customer expectations shift, and you will be stuck with them for a long time if you don't actively update them. If it is too expensive to carry out, think about other solutions: find MVPs, cut it into digestible pieces, turn it around, and take it personally. In your house from the 1930's this is the toilet in the outhouse—do not accept a shortfall here. You do not want to walk to the outhouse through the snow in the middle of the night—there should be zero tolerance policy here. The ones in the

bottom left corner, you shouldn't bother too much with

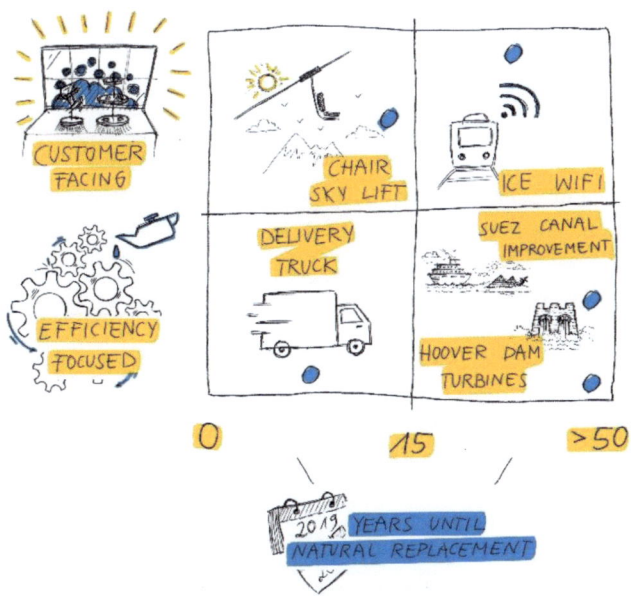

They have little downside potential, and after a short period of time, you'll get another shot. All you need to do is make sure that the next generation is actually amazing. In your house from the 1930's, this is the old fridge.

Things that are Customer Facing but should get replaced relatively soon are found in the

top left corner, and subject to case-by-case evaluation

Characteristics that suggest an immediate replacement of the outdated component are as follows:

- High risk of sudden shift in customer expectation
- Small cost of improvement
- New generation offers greater future flexibility

If none of these apply, it is advisable not to replace your hardware. In your house, these are the new tiles in the bathroom. If you can make it significantly nicer with just a little amount of money, do it. If it would require great effort, wait until you renovate the bathroom anyway.

Hardware Legacies in the

bottom right corner are subject to a simple business case

between the expected efficiency gain and the cost of investment. They are Efficiency Focused and in long use; replace, if it is a good financial deal. In your house, this is new wall insulation.

If you do decide to invest in a replacement of Customer-Facing hardware, make sure you don't run into the same mistake again. The new hardware needs to be modern at the time of delivery, not 5 years ago when the project started, even in details like the colors chosen.

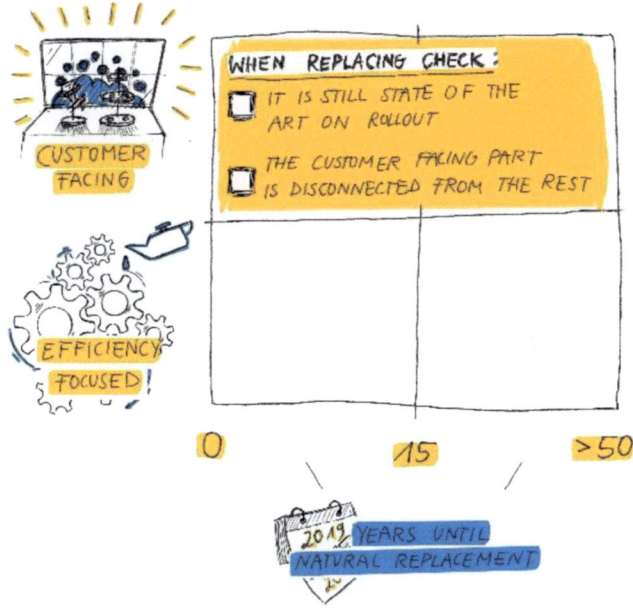

Also, the next generation should allow for updates on the Customer-Facing part, with little effort required.

Legacy IT

It sounds odd to talk about IT and legacies in the same chapter, as digitalization is usually the solution to old-fashioned processes, not the source of them.

But as a matter of fact, many established businesses have entangled themselves with dozens—sometimes even hundreds—of IT systems that are ageing.

If these systems are strongly connected with others, it is risky and complicated to update them. This way, the decision is usually evaded and postponed—after all, the systems are running, aren't they? But

"Never change a running system" makes you a dinosaur in 5 years

Very soon you will discover that the operating systems, databases, firewalls and even the necessary hardware will become first outdated, then no longer supported, and finally not available anymore.

As a result, you will not be able to introduce any new features, as the system you are running is essentially a zombie—neither dead nor alive. You will also experience a difficult time recruiting engineers capable of coding anything in such a system. In fact, it would be a dead-end street in their career, too, dealing with outdated technology.

Having coded myself in the late 1990's, I saw the panic in the managements' eyes when they were desperately looking for people to check legacy codes for potential Y2K bugs in programming languages that, by that time, hadn't been used in many years, formats such as Lisp, Fortran or Cobol.

Only constant maintenance saves you from this. When looking at the business case, it is important not to fall short on ambition, because:

Killing one legacy component is a negative case, while modernizing the system is a positive case

Only if you can really get rid of all the complexity costs of running an old system is it worth making the effort. If you only spend money on modernizing some aspects of the code base, but you keep up with the complexity of the old world, you will have only succeeded in making it even more complex: you will have added more systems to a still complex legacy environment.

How to recognize an IT legacy system? Let's take a look at an example and derive the characteristics from thereon.

In the 1970's, Deutsche Bahn used a reservation system called EPA. It grew into a European solution that other rail companies either used or which their IT systems could at least communicate with.

This way, an increasing number of features and interfaces were added, for example, pricing features.

A sophisticated IT-hardware infrastructure allowed for the rapid transmission of reservation data to dedicated printers in train depots, which would then print out seat reservation signs to be placed on trains by conductors. This process was later even adapted to the discs that set the electronic signs on the train.

With all these features, it became a core part of the distribution system, even when an update called Kurs 90 was introduced.

The problems became obvious when yield management systems were introduced everywhere. Deutsche Bahn also introduced such a system in 2002.

The yield system did not replace the seat reservations—it simply seemed too complex to rebuild all the features EPA had established over a period of 20 years. As a result, there were two parallel systems doing very similar things—both capable of counting the bookings on a train, and both capable of pricing.

The result was a range of ridiculous contradictions visible to the customers. For example, the yield system would expect low demand and offered cheap fares, but the reservation system was booked out, suggesting the train was over-crowded. This would also work the other way around: you could have paid for a high-price train when there were still many seats available.

Moreover, other outside constraints had changed. Train configurations became less predictable. For example, there were three different setups, with different capacities, of ICE 1 trains. By the time it was finally clear which train was to be used for a given ride, it was too late to enter the correct configuration into the reservation system quickly. This resulted in only the smallest common denominator of all configurations being bookable. This issue was only solved when the train setup was finally unified. Keep this example in mind when reading point 4 of the following list of 7 characteristics of systems causing significant damage.

Also, there was no online connection to the trains, which meant that reservations had to be made before the initial departure of a train, which could have been many hours before reaching a particular station on the route.

Finally, the numbering system always consisted of two leading digits labeling the "compartment" and a third digit labeling the seat number.

As a result, numbers ending in 0 or 9 could not be used, as no "compartment" had a seat number 0 or more than 8 seats in total; the system did not allow it.

When the IC Busses went into operation years later, the seats had to be re-labeled from their logical order to this incomprehensible compartment system.

Finally, the decision was made to replace the reservation system in 2017—after 40 years of being in operation.

From this example, you can find the following characteristics:

1. *The original system is over 10 years old*

2. *Many features have been added that were not part of the original design*

3. *The system is deeply integrated with other applications*

4. *It is easier to fix the operational hardware/processes to fit the system than it is to do things the other way around*

5. *Replacing the system with a newer version appears to be extremely complex*

6. *The system's features overlap with newer systems*

7. *The user's experience is affected by the system's shortfalls*

Count the checks on your list; this will help you prioritize in terms of where you should start.

If you have 5 or more, you need to act immediately. This system is causing significant damage to your business.

With 3 or 4 checks, you should begin to develop a strategy for the next generation. With 1 or 2, you should merely put it on a watchlist.

Finally, the question of how to update the system remains. After all, the complexity of changing it was one of the most important reasons for not starting it in the past. This will be the subject of the next chapter.

Programming a wholly new and independent software tool in parallel with an outdated IT system and then switching when it is ready is something that is tempting on many levels.

You don't need to understand the old system and can focus on the new features, you can cut off all the technological dept built up over the decades, and it usually doesn't take a long time to do it when you use modern methods.

There is one very important reason, however, for this usually still not being the best option:

Any new software needs to be deployed 12 months after specifying it, at the latest

If this doesn't happen, realities will have changed by the time you deploy it, and the new software will be outdated on delivery. You would have to manage a simultaneous process of adapting the old system to changes as well as the specs of the one in development, without ever really putting it to the test, over the course of more than a year—that is bound to go terribly wrong.

There is usually no chance of having it replaced within 12 months, especially if you are talking about big, complex legacy IT systems. Therefore, you need to:

Find pieces that you can take out and replace one by one

I'll present three basic strategies for creating pieces small enough to be replaced.

This strategy is aimed at creating sub-units in the system in focus. A code is usually designed in some kind of substructure anyway.

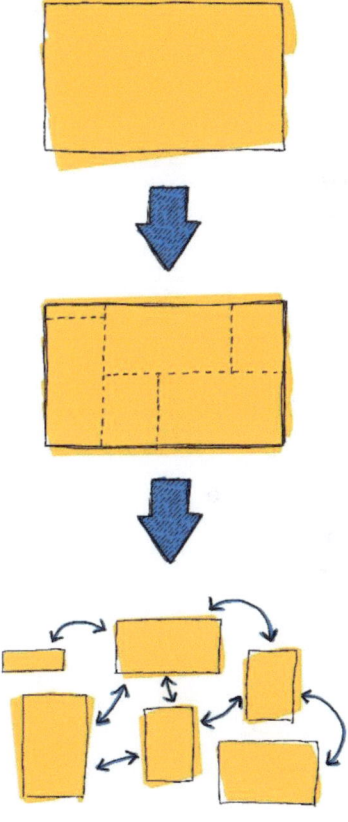

Following these lines, it is often possible to clean up the inter-tangled parts, and instead obtain a clear communication of the separated units through defined interfaces.

Once this has taken place, it is possible to replace every independent piece of code with new technology using the defined interfaces. The pieces can be very small. Even if at first glance, cutting out small pieces doesn't seem to be adding much in the way of progress, it is significant. As code complexity works exponentially with the number of involved interdependencies, even reducing the interdependencies by 1 has a great effect on the rest.

This approach is especially recommendable if safety-relevant and comfort-relevant components are entangled in one system. They need to be separated, because if the comfort-relevant components have to be approved by protocols of safety features, innovation slows down.

One example of this is an elevator. You should decouple the display system from the general operation system, allowing you to update your customer-facing displays to the latest fashion, style, color and usability, without having to homologate the safety of the entire system.

Quite frequently, you will find more modern systems that have an interface with the old one you'd like to replace. One option for cutting down the complexity of your legacy system therefore

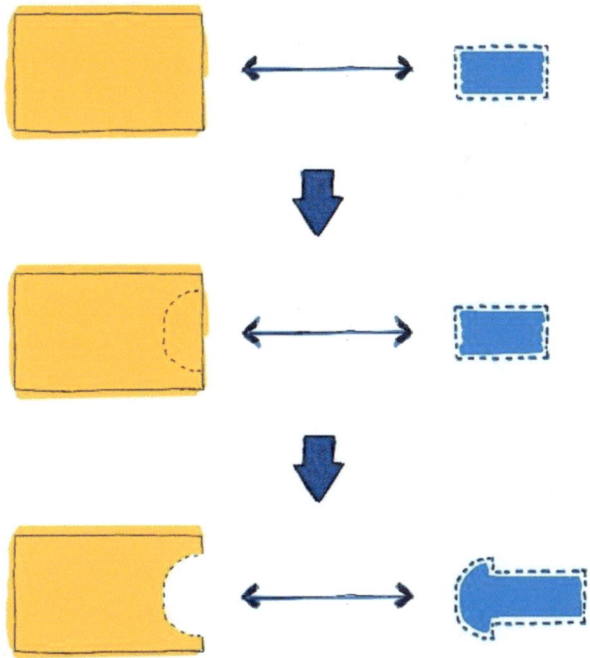

involves integrating that part of the old system (the one which interacts with the new one) into the new system. Often, the definition of which system is leading, and which one is using data is free to be defined. To a certain extent, all that needs to be done is to change the ownership of the data. Referring to the example above, the moment at which the new yield management system was deployed, there was a chance to move ownership of booking data and reservation processes into this new system.

Of course, this shift of responsibilities also requires clean interfaces, just as with the Inner Cut, but a well-designed overtaking system is still usually better at providing these.

The last segmentation strategy involves creating a small nucleolus in the system—one which is independent from the rest.

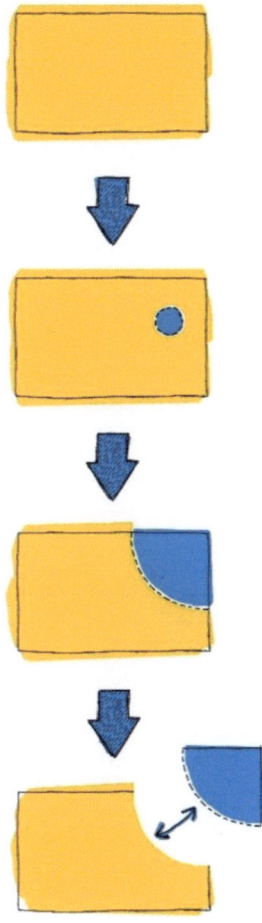

After having done so, an increasing number of functions are moved into this part of the code. Once the size is significant, you can cut it out and replace it in the same way as the other cases.

Of course, it is both possible and realistic to apply a combination of all three strategies. When doing so, however, there is the demand for an overarching software-architecture concept, so always be sure to choose the best strategy.

(Legal) Regulations
The three Types of Regulations

Why do regulations form part of the chapter on legacies? This is because they usually are—however, they are disguised as unchangeable, given constraints.

In many cases, if you want to change a process in your system quickly, the reason stopping you from doing so is: *"This does not comply with regulation XY."*

If you recall what we are looking for from the beginning of this chapter (*[...] you need to get rid of all the things around you that are hindering you from being fast [...]*), regulations need to be addressed.

How can you address something that appears to be set in stone? It is helpful to group the rules into blocks. You can generally find the following three types:

- Implicit legal regulations
- Explicit legal regulations
- Company internal regulations

The first reflex is normally as follows:

a) that most regulations come under the purview of the first two groups, and

b) therefore are next to impossible to change.

But in my experience, both parts of this reflex are incorrect.

You will find a surprising number of rule-sets that corporations have given themselves over the years in all kinds of areas, but most of all in operations.

The reason for this is that, unlike departments that were born in modern working environments like yield management or SEO marketing, operations typically has a long history.

In this history, the leadership style of choice was usually hierarchical, and following orders set by a superior often ended in long manuals on how exactly to execute things. This tradition is difficult to overcome, as some of the rules are safety related protocols—you can't just abandon them; still, it pays to reconsider them.

Here is a great opportunity to invite business outsiders, pensioners, family members or children to ask you, at every step of the routine, again and again: Why? Why? Why?

Ask yourself if things really are written in any law

When going open-mindedly through your ruleset, you will find that explicit legal regulations are very rare. Laws have to apply to an entire nation, or even internationally, over decades or centuries.
They simply can't always address the specific process you are dealing with. At best, they can do it on a very high level.

Therefore, a practice of implicit legal regulations was established. People started to work in a certain way in order to translate the blurry legal regulations into their particular case. Sometimes, this is backed by court sentences, but most of the times not even by that.

As a result, you will find most of the rules you're following in the non-legally binding categories. We'll look at examples of all three types and introduce strategies to increase the level of freedom for each one.

I'd like to start with the above-mentioned regulations, because they are frequently confused with explicit legal regulations.

The reason for this is that, in most companies, there are procedures meant to comply with laws, while in reality it is an internal assumption of how to do this—not explicitly stated in any law. This is a very important difference, because for implicit legal regulations you

don't change the law, but your internal process related to it

A fine example of this are work safety instructions. German law states that employers have to instruct their employees in workplace safety after hiring them, and after any significant change to the work environment.

The standard procedure for complying with this in a non-critical work habitat—such as an office space—is to call all employees together, attend a short classroom training session on it, and then have them sign a protocol to show that they have participated.

The problem with this is that it never works. Somebody always misses the training either because they were on holiday, sick, on a business trip, or simply forgot about it. Even with five repetitions of the session, you will always have somebody missing. Even if you eventually manage to get everybody to complete it, three new hires might enter your company, and then the game starts all over again.

The mistake here is that nowhere in the law does it say: "Have a classroom training session which people attend." This is the internal interpretation. As a matter of fact, it is perfectly fine to conduct an online tutorial which employees have to enter and pass. Having this, you can even automatically track and chase down the ones who keep forgetting about it. The trainer only makes a one-off effort in producing the tutorial. If the work environment changes, simply update the tutorial.

Strategy number one is therefore convincing and simple to state, but takes a great amount of effort to bring to life:

Limit internal rules to the very core—and then do it again

You are not alone. Others have the same problems and do the same things. At the peak of refugee migration to Europe in 2015/2016, police were told by their governments to reintroduce border procedures within the Schengen area.

One of the explicit regulations here is that even within the Schengen area, everybody needs to have a valid passport or ID card when crossing a border.

The police interpreted this as a form of implication, in that bus operators crossing borders are obliged to check the passports of all their clients. Consequently, they planned to impose fines on operators not "complying" with their internal interpretation of the law.
However, it was impossible to comply with it, as bus drivers neither had the authority nor the necessary training to check several hundred potential document types for validity at a bus-stop without any infrastructure to carry out such a process.

Does an Australian citizen require a visa to travel from Italy to Switzerland? Even representatives of the Ministry of the Interior couldn't answer that question correctly when we asked them; how should a bus driver do it?

It took over two years to finally get a sentence from the European supreme court which declared this police interpretation of the law void.

To transfer this to a more general level, you will often find outside regulations which affect your business, such as airport regulations affecting airlines, parking regulations affecting taxi services, smoking regulations affecting pubs, and so on.

If you really believe that an outside interpretation of a law is wrong and hinders you,

take it to court and have a judge look at it

If your assumption was correct, the judge will most likely follow your line of argument. However, be prepared for the fact that the sentence might be unfavorable too. In that case, taking it to court forces you to comply with something you wanted to leave behind.

Despite this given risk, it pays to actively approach questionable outside rules.

Explicit Legal Regulations

After you have put all the Implicit Legal Regulations into the correct bucket, you are left with very few Explicit Legal Regulations relevant for your business.

When looking through these, sort out the ones that are identical and fair for all competitors, potential intruders, and disrupters.
Common examples here are taxes, working-time regulations, and environmental standards.

However, keep in mind that there can be unbalanced rules between competitors even in this area, like the missing fuel tax for kerosene, which gives the airline industry a competitive advantage over land-based modes of transportation.

Focus on the legal regulations with competitive implications

In this group, answer the following two questions:

1. How big is the business impact?

2. How old-fashioned/outdated is the regulation?

Plot them on a chart like this:

Let's look at some examples, starting with the top-right quadrant

'Large business impact and obviously outdated'

In the public's perception, the rise of the German long-distance coach market came as a consequence of the (legal) liberalization of the market in January 2013. Few people are aware of the fact that the first two companies—DeinBus and MeinFernbus—had already started in 2011 and 2012 respectively under the old legislation.

For them, the question of liberalization had the biggest possible business effect. At the same time, the law from the

1930's prohibiting coach lines (apart from a few dedicated exceptions) was ridiculously outdated.

Nobody I talked to, including profiteers of the old regulation, could name a single good reason as to why it would be smart to prohibit long-distance coach services in Germany.

This combination could be leveraged, and the two companies did it with on several levels that are applicable to comparable situations.

For one, they simply applied for concessions anyway, taking the cases to court—a strategy already mentioned in the chapter above on implicit legal regulations. Here, they found judges who also thought the regulations were serving no just purpose. As the company's lawyers found loopholes in the existing regulations, they were more than happy to follow this line of argument.

Second, they managed to play to the public's perception of this very cleverly, because not only was the story very entertaining but also easily understandable.

Finally, they were in a favorable political position and managed to place their demand at the right time and with the right allies.

Ironically, only one of the two (MeinFernbus, who later merged with FlixBus) benefited from this success. DeinBus practically disappeared from the market soon after.

What they did correctly was to

Focus on the one great story, and play it everywhere

DeinBus, however, forgot to

Prepare for when you actually achieve what you want

because that can happen unexpectedly and quickly. Put only one regulation in this quadrant: Don't play with more topics at once. This would dilute your efforts and ultimately get you nowhere.

Obviously, there is not much to say about the bottom-left:

'Small business impact and, in parts, up-to-date'

Just don't bother. These parts can be annoying and strange at times, but learn to live with them. An example of this is the fact that every company that wants to apply for coach concessions in Germany needs to own at least one bus. If you have a shared economy approach like FlixBus, the buses are the property of partner companies. FlixBus holds the concession, but has no need for a bus, other than to comply with this regulation. The simple solution was to buy one used bus and put it in a garage—problem solved.

Don't waste your energy

This situation is different if you are in the bottom-right quadrant

'Large business impact and, in parts, up to date'

The big difference when compared to the top-right quadrant

is that the story-telling is not as easy or entertaining.

You need an institution people trust

to make up for the interesting story that is missing. These things take time, and I'd like to refer to an example from the mid-1970's.

The maximum speed for buses in Germany at that time was 80 km/h. This was a significant competitive disadvantage for the product, given that cars had gotten faster since the 1950's. However, fatalities in traffic peaked in 1975, and even if there was no connection to buses, it was a difficult environment in which to trigger a discussion about raising the maximum speed to 100 km/h.

The solution to this was to convince the administration to conduct a project evaluating the risks of raising the speed limit within the "Bundesanstalt für Straßenwesen," a scientific department of the ministry of transportation.

These people were considered experts and came up with a couple of technical criteria that would qualify buses for testing a higher top speed. This started in 1977; by 1979, half of the newly manufactured buses met the criteria and were therefore approved to be part of the 100 km/h test. According to the institution, the result suggested there was neither a negative impact on safety nor on traffic flow. Thus the Ministry of Transportation approved the 100 km/h under the stated technical conditions, which very soon practically all the buses met. The investigation proved to be right, as there was no negative effect on safety.

This remained so for almost 30 years, until finally 100km/h also became the legal standard, no longer the exception, in 2007.

If you think about the quadrant on the top left:

'Small business impact and obviously outdated'

you could argue that you should not waste your energy here either. Align yourself with the given situation and live with it. There is one difference here though.
These cases have a story that everybody understands easily. Even if there is no value in pushing all the buttons to make it heard, it pays to tell it to a select audience, such as authorities, experts, or industry-congresses.

The moment might come at which the regulations are altered, anyway, for another reason.

Wait for this moment to address the outdated regulation

An appropriate example of this is the obligation to carry original paper copies of the concessions for bus lines on the bus itself. These copies are neither forgery-proof, nor is there any way for a policeman checking a coach to tell if the document in his hand is still valid. It is quite a logistical effort for authorities and bus operators all over Europe to manage these documents. They need to be registered, shipped and tracked across the continent, and if you need to switch two buses between two lines, you need to ensure the concession documents are switched too.

Finally, think about keeping a document in the glove

compartment of a car for years, one which several thousand people have access to: drivers, customers, cleaning-staff, and garage personnel. Would you put your wallet there?

A much smarter solution would be a central database which contains all the concessions issued. Any policeman would immediately check if it is valid, and any change would be available, instantly, for everybody. There would be no more demand for big cupboards filled with paper. It would be more effective and more efficient for authorities as well as operators.

Still the status quo is not threatening the business model, and therefore there is time to wait for the next update of the corresponding regulation.

Company Internal Regulations

It is amazing how many you find out there, and it is surprising how many of those are unknown or even ignored. Indeed, you find companies possessing innumerable books about them.

When a colleague of mine at Deutsche Bahn incorporated a new rule into the internal rule book, the editor told her that she was now an immortal part of company history, as her rule is now part of this document and always will be.

It is not surprising that internal regulation books and Industry 4.0 don't go together very well. What you need is a regular revision of all your internal rules.

Step 1 involves finding them all, because they are often hidden

Places to look for them are:

1. Explicit rule books

2. Manuals

3. Training materials

4. Terms and conditions

5. Approval procedures in relation to procurement, travel, and so on

6. Official documents such as HR feedback forms, expenses forms, and so on

Look in every corner. If you have transparency, the most ridiculous ones will jump out immediately. Outdated rules and transparency are natural enemies.

I remember that in 2009 I still had to fill out an internal form explaining why my new hire required access to the Internet at work. He then had to fill out several pages of disclaimers, promising to not use it for private purposes. This statement had to be updated on a regular basis.

This single example might seem funny and unimportant, but it's the volume that matters. You keep a great share of your creative potential busy with procedures which add no value, and end up slowing down the organization.

It becomes even more critical if internal processes are a reason not to do something that would add value. This could be procurement regulations that keep you from buying something, that would have a big business impact, or that is an approval that is needed in the process by Mr. Bottleneck, who just doesn't answer.

Step 2 is about attaching a best-before date to every internal rule

Rules need to be revised on a regular basis. In a fast-moving world, anything over two years old should be checked for relevance. This only happens if rules are automatically void after two years, so you are forced to think about them.

This will prompt a significant change in the culture too, as there will be a discussion held on justifying the prolongation of an internal rule, rather than having to justify an attempt to cancel it. That is exactly the shift you need.

Also, people writing manuals will seriously reconsider their volume if they have to reassess them themselves every other year.

TRANSLATING OPERATIONS INTO IT REQUIREMENTS

In many businesses, operations and IT are miles apart on many levels. They often represent opposite ends of the scale.

Quite frequently you'll find, for instance, the lowest average age in IT and the highest in operations.

You often find nerdishly brilliant, single, science fiction fans with top university degrees in IT, and down-to-earth football fans supporting their teenage children in operations.

Also, the workplaces usually look completely different in terms of the following: clothes they wear; 24/7 shift work vs. office work; the level of interest in company strategy; the attitude towards unions; language skills and number of nationalities in teams, and so on

How are they to find a common ground? Well, finding it is indeed what you need to do if you want to stand any chance of digitalizing your operations.

That is the purpose of this chapter. It is meant to be a guide on how to bridge the gap and identify the potential.

The Operations Mantra

This entire book is based on the topic of digitalizing and automating operational processes. As industries are often very specific, it is impossible to offer one solution to each and every situation out there, even if a lot of examples are provided.

However, there is a generic pattern you should be looking for, which I refer to as my Operations Mantra.

A digital operations process always begins with collecting all available data from all available sources; of course, this needs to happen automatically. The data has to be relevant to decisions and reliable.

This could be the temperatures of components, usage rates of clients, weather forecasts, or GPS positions; anything you need to make an educated decision. When looking for these, start with the KPIs and a report you frequently look at, if you want to get an idea of how your organization is performing.

The second step involves defining which part of the decisions that the data suggests is simple and straightforward, and which part is complex. The majority of cases should belong to the straightforward category. An easy example is as follows: your data point is the temperature in a sauna. If it is under x°, you should heat it up again—straightforward.

The straightforward cases should be resolved by the system automatically. In the above example, you should have an automatic heating system, not a human turning up the heat.

For the complex cases, the system should offer priority to users, in order to lead them to the most important cases for a decision first.

In the sauna example, if the temperature drop in some saunas is unusually fast (indicating a gap in the insulation), the system should provide a list to the janitor, showing which one is cooling down the fastest, who would start by repairing that one.

Finally following a manual decision, the execution of the decision should be taken over by the system again.

If, in the sauna case, the most frequent reason for a drop in temperature is an open door, you could consider a remote option for the janitor to close it without having to go to the door.

I would now like to move from this small example to a much larger one, but where the same principle applies.

Think of the question of bus delays. These can occur anywhere and at anytime, as traffic flow is not constant and traffic jams can occur.

DATA IS COLLECTED (SEMI-) AUTOMATICALLY FROM ALL AVAILABLE SOURCES

80% Simple — PREPROCESS — 20% Complex

FULL AUTOMATIC

PROVIDE PRIO

EXECUTE

IT SUPPORT HANDLING

SOLUTION

The ideal process for handling this is to:

1. Collect all available data such as:

   a. the real time GPS position of the bus

   b. forecast of the traffic situation for the remaining trip

   c. contact information of clients

   d. and others

2. Divide the delays you find into small and large delays automatically

3. For the:

   a. small delays, inform clients about the delay and provide them with real-time GPS information

   b. large delays, order them by severity and present them to a dispatcher. If he, for example, decides to rebook clients, the system will automatically execute this decision and inform the clients

There exists an endless list of examples from all kinds of applications. Think of predictive maintenance screening engine data to predict the ideal replacement moment for a component, using weather correlations when predicting demand curves in a café, and so on.

The greatest challenge is to identify the manual processes and design the mantra process. And when you're done, do it again. Or, to stay with the example of delay management, why not automate the rebooking decision in 3.b. using rules as well?

Digital Operation Leaders
Who do you find

The most important reason for companies struggling or even failing to digitalize their business is that the management does not understand it.

The skills required for management positions in operations were for the longest time as follows:

- Capability of dealing with large teams and multiple layers of sub-structures

- Managing people you never see (because they work elsewhere or on the night-shift)

- Deep understanding of operational processes

- Delivering reliable quality on established procedures

- Speaking the language of down-to-earth staff

The typical profile you will find in these positions is therefore 45–65 year-olds; often the older they are, the higher up they are. There are two typical career paths.

Either they started as a simple employee, proved talented, then took over a little team, gained experience—sometimes attending universities alongside their job—became the first officer of a larger division, and after many years, at the age of 50, took it over. That is usually also the limit to how far this group can go.

The other group is composed of academics who entered operations after a few years elsewhere at a lieutenant level, then stayed because they enjoyed the practical part of things. They are typically a little younger when entering higher positions as they had a head start, but the difference is slim because they too need to learn how to address a large group of people in an appropriate language, build expertise in their area, and so on...all of which takes time.

There are some cases in which top management operations positions are assigned to a high-potential outsider. However, they are usually fairly disconnected to their underbodies and don't stay long enough to make a significant difference before their way to the top calls again.

When aiming to bring digital skills into your leadership team, you can't have a big bang. The skills relevant in the past remain important, at least, in a transition phase. You need to find people who have the skills described above, and on top of this, the right digital mindset.

You need somebody who is able to understand and manage the status quo, but at the same time also able to turn it upside down.

The biggest challenge by far—especially for established businesses—is to find the right leaders

from this pool of candidates.

Who are you looking for?

As operations is often not very good at promoting itself internally or externally, you find lots of people within operations who have managed to automate some annoying process and then never talked about it. Make that a focus when screening candidates. You should look for

people who can automate a process

Find people who left their comfort zones before, and have experience in other industries, countries and careers. These people are

curious, open minded, and embrace change

In an ideal portfolio, you will find somebody who has experienced

some software development period in their life

Particularly in mechanical industries, there are a surprisingly large quantity of people such as an engineer who ran a little software project back in university.

However, the number is limited, and this is definitely a battle for talents you have to win. The advantage you possess is that these skills are often hidden, because they were not required for the longest time—you are digging for gold nuggets rather than browsing in a jewelry store.

The first step toward digitalizing your operations is to form a leadership team within your organization, in which every single member:

1. Loathes repetitive, manual processes

2. Is capable of writing an IT requirement that IT can understand

3. Can keep the status quo running

If there are several layers of hierarchy, this needs to hold true for the top two of them at least—ideally all the way down to the team-leader level. Of course, you need to start at the top.

Go to a retreat with all the top-level leaders in operations

Tell them about your general goal of turning every repetitive, manual process in your organization into an automated routine executed by machines. Use the reasoning from the chapter on business potential from Operations 4.0. Inform them about the mantra.

It will be a very emotional moment, because it will question everything they had been doing so far.

But it will also be a tell-tale moment. There will be people who are intrigued by the idea, people who will totally oppose it, and the cautious rest.

You will probably be flooded with examples that can't be

automated and the reasons for it. This is the perfect starting point. Pick them up in a brainstorm and plot them on a chart like this:

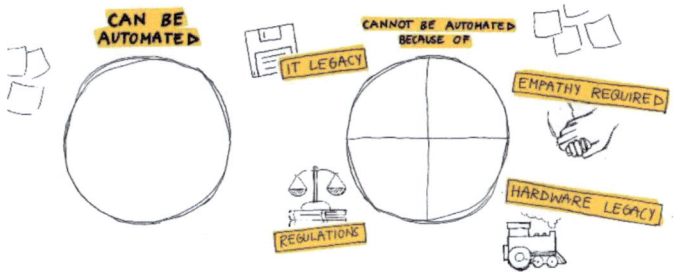

These boards will, of course, look very different depending on your particular situation. The following examples should help you to give an idea of the general nature of each field.

Ski resort example

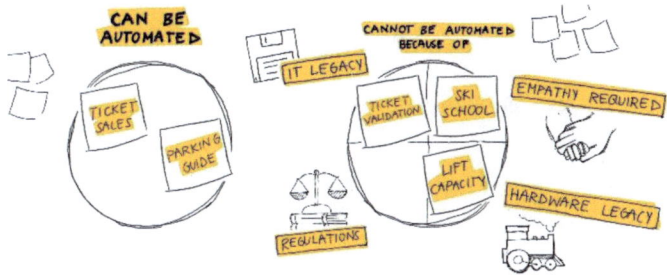

Call center example

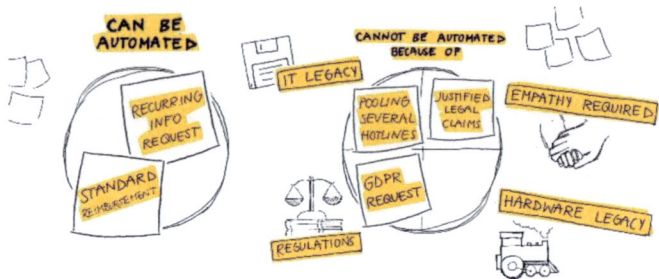

After you have collected them, challenge them together. Move them around until there is a certain level of consensus that the picture is accurate. The only processes allowed to remain manual are the ones that require empathy. For the others, you will find strategies to overcome them in the chapter on legacies.

Share these strategies with your leaders, and make them come up with the detailed first drafts of automation goal roadmaps for their field of responsibility, taking the items from the chart you have just filled in.

The idea of the roadmap will be introduced in detail in the next chapter.

Referring to the first examples, it could look somewhat like this:

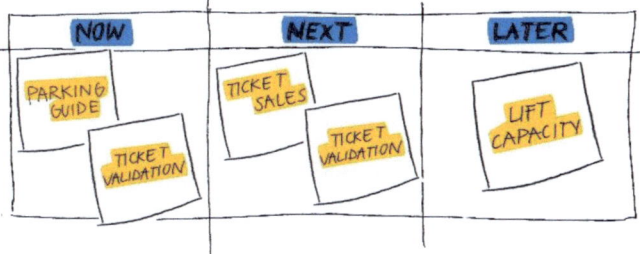

After this, some time is required. Everybody will need a chance to familiarize themselves with their thoughts. As they are logical and convincing, the chances are your leaders will understand. Make that a constant item on the agenda for your one-on-ones with them.

Three groups will be formed after this process.

1. Leaders who are embracing the realistic road into the digital future of what they do—chock-full of initiatives

2. Leaders who see the necessity but feel challenged, and wonder if they can actually be helpful in that process

3. Leaders who continue to refuse the approach, claiming it had always worked well without it

You need to quickly empower the first group and train the second.
Leaders stuck in group 3 cannot be part of your operations anymore if you truly want to make it digital. You will need to find replacements. Look for the above criteria when screening new candidates.

As soon as you have adequate confidence that your top leaders have understood and have internalized the need for the road to automation, have them start the same process within their teams. Take a more passive role in these retreats, unless they take off in a completely wrong direction.

Operational IT

Equally important as developing operations' ability to articulate what they need to automate for IT is establishing a deep understanding of operations within IT. You need to set up the structures and responsibilities within IT too.

Product Domains

The best way for this is to set up dedicated IT teams—usually referred to as *'product domains'* within IT. Each should be responsible for one dedicated area of operations and for their own piece of IT code, as described in the chapter on Legacy IT.

As a matter of fact, the IT setup should also follow the operations setup on a structural level.

Each department in operations should have an IT team

If that is not possible, because IT systems are too deeply integrated with others, this is the first task IT needs to solve.

Decouple operations-related source code by following the organizational setup in operations

As a resulting setup, each operations department should have 'their' IT team, and each IT team 'their' operations department.

If possible, look for volunteers within the IT department to sign up for these domains. To do so, the department leaders from operations should take the time to explain the top-level roadmap you developed in your retreat. This has to be a sales pitch, explaining the vision and goals, which could also prove to be an interesting exercise for the department leaders.

Product Owner and Business Owner

In this setup, both teams need an entry point for the other, because it is just as hard to find IT people able to relate to operational needs, as it is to find operations people able to articulate IT requirements.

Dedicate one person on each team to being this interface for the other

In the domain approach, these are often referred to as *Product Owners* (IT) and *Business Owners* (Operations). At least for the first year,

the Business Owner needs to be the Head of the Operations Department

If you allow a delegation in the team too early, your leaders might be tempted to avoid the necessary transition of their own work.

A great part of the success of your new setup depends on the quality of the relation between your IT teams and your operations teams. Foster this relationship as much as possible.

A positive attitude toward the other team is a pre-requisite for both

If prejudices survive (*'what do these IT nerds know about real life?'* vs. *'these ops people just don't understand the modern world'*), you will fail.

In order to be successful, you need to create moments at which both teams actually see what the other is doing.

Put the IT developers on a locomotive for a day, have them scoop the ice-cream ball, and put them on the counters, levers and steering wheels. When doing so, cover them up, so that there's always somebody by their side to help them should they get in trouble.
This exercise it not meant to prove to them that your prejudice was right,

it is meant to excite IT about the beauty of Operations

The examples I have witnessed had immediate impact. When we applied this for the first time it took just one day, as there was great astonishment within the IT team at how features are applied in the field (often enough not as designed). There was also a long list of (super) quick fixes and ideas about the further steps devised by the developers.

In turn, have operations people join in on IT's daily routines. You will be surprised at how rarely they have ever met anyone who is using what they do. Take your time and show them, answer questions, and explain. Then spend a day with them too.

They have routines unknown to operations. Let them explain their tools, work, and meeting modes. Make them explain their challenges and strong holds—this is again a challenge for IT, because they have to explain complicated things in simple language. This is the moment for avoiding stereotypes on their side. Afterwards,

operations should understand what IT can do easily and what is complex

This will later help to focus on those requirements that deliver the biggest gains with the smallest effort.
It is therefore important for operations to get a feeling about the complexity drivers and how to avoid them.

Roadmap Approach

Operations typically concerns a lot of complicated details that need to come together to deliver a product. In this complexity, very few people actually possess a solid understanding about what is going on.

It is even more difficult to judge if the initiatives and projects within operations are heading in the right direction, and if they are sufficiently ambitious to achieve the company goals.

This situation is not so different from old-school IT working in waterfall projects. Without delving too deep into this, it is a management scheme that consists of a sequence of steps which always have to be followed in that exact order:

1. IT concept

2. deciding on budget and priorities

3. IT design plan

4. coding components

5. testing components

6. merging components

7. testing the merger

8. deploying the release

It often takes years to get a requirement through this process.

Furthermore, only very few people, if any, understand what is really going on, and whether the general development is heading in the desired direction.

Within IT, the solution for this is the introduction of several agile methods, basically aiming at breaking IT development down into small but viable pieces and place them on an easily comprehensible table of priorities, often referred to as a roadmap. These are then handled in a totally open manner.

In many offices, you even find them pasted on the wall. This results in full transparency, so that now even non-IT stakeholders are able to discuss the priorities and pieces which, in turn, increases the quality of the output.

Experiencing the same challenges as old-school IT, it is obvious that the same solutions should be applied in operations as well

Start with the roadmaps you got from the retreat with your department leaders in the last chapter and use them as agile roadmaps.

The most important difference is usually cutting the general goals up into small, viable steps together with the teams. Team involvement marks another important success factor in the transition.

This takes some practice, and if your organization is not familiar with this kind of approach, there is expertise out there which can help in this step. Search for 'agile coaches' and you'll find a great number to choose from.

Once the roadmaps are there, make them public and discuss them with all your stakeholders—one of the most important ones being the dedicated IT teams.

This will be a new experience for operations staff, as they were used to nobody really understanding what they did.

It is transparency that will open the door to change

Still be prepared to deal with defensive battles within your team, with some people not wanting to publish what they do. Allow some time for a transition, but don't tolerate full opposition here for longer than a few weeks, or it will inhibit the change in general.

Finally, when you have roadmaps that are backed by your operations teams, agreed upon by outside stakeholders and aligned with IT and with their roadmaps, you have changed the structure of the work and most of its deficits.

1. You have published tasks that are achievable, in contrast to only being able to fail before

2. You have a list of very concrete steps on the way to automation—it is a process, not a bang

3. The organization around you have a clear picture of what you are doing and thus:

4. You have a real chance of finding outside talents to be part of this operations

To conclude this transition and make it irreversible, you need to make sure this way of working is a structural element of your company culture, which will be the topic of the next chapter.

MANAGING THE CHANGE IN YOUR TEAM

We've already touched on some potential reactions from people involved in the transition process and how to deal with them, but this was just the tip of the iceberg. What you need is a holistic strategy on the topic of HR in your operations.

You could even go as far as saying that:

With the right team, digitalization is inevitable

If you imagine a team structure full of hungry leaders desperate to modernize the daily routine because they themselves are annoyed by it and backed by a team fully committed to this goal, proactively coming up with solutions for how to get there, how could you stop the transition, even if you wanted to?

Involving HR and Recruiting

One of the most important internal partners for the transition to a digitalized operations environment is human resources.

They need to be involved in three very important parts of the process, and they also need to be capable of actually delivering added value, which might require some training or change processes on the HR side too.

The first part is the hiring.

All new hires on all levels must have a digital attitude

There have been some aspects on this in the chapter on digital leaders, and more detail will be provided in the following segment on hiring principles.

Second, they need to provide

support on the new management tools like roadmaps

This is an area in which outside knowledge might be required. HR will only have the resources to provide this kind of support to the leadership level.

They will then have to act as multiplicators in the team, making it even more important to have their buy-in. This is addressed in the segment on change for existing leaders.

Finally, there is a shift in what kind of behavior is valuable to a digital operations (innovative, disruptive, and so on) compared to old-school operations (delivering constantly identical results, duplicating processes, and so on)

New values require new evaluation (tools)

This needs to be reflected on many levels. For a simple start, you need to tell them about it, but you will also need new and different communication, as well as feedback and innovation schemes.

All of this will require a change in corresponding tools and meeting formats. This is in the content of the segment on change at the team level.

Finally, there is a very important question which is as delicate as it is important, and therefore needs to be addressed pro-actively:

Will the automations result in layoffs?

There is no simple yes or no answer, but—to wrap up the following segment on balancing efficiency gains and job security—in most cases, the impact is not immediate and can be managed in a way in which those affected are left with options.

Hiring Principles

If you want to change the attitude of the team within operations toward a digital mindset, you absolutely need to ensure that all employees entering the organization, at all levels, bring this skill.

If you recall the qualities for leaders from the chapter on digital leaders, they should be:

- people who can automate a process
- curious, open minded, and embrace change
- experienced a software-development period in their life

There is only a slight adjustment for team members:

- people who actively question a manual process
- curious, open minded, and embrace change
- some software affinity in their life

When recruiting new leaders, you will also need to make sure they are capable of managing the status quo. These skills are hard to find in one person, but you need them. In addition, you should look for:

- experience in managing (very) big units with sub-team structures
- significant experience on the area of responsibility

This is a significant challenge for recruiting, because it drastically reduces the number of potential candidates in a competitive hiring environment.

There are a few necessary changes that will help to address this issue.

HR needs adequate resources to actively approach talents

rather than waiting for incoming applications. As this will be a constant challenge, this needs to be set up in-house. These recruiters then need to track potential candidates through all kinds of networks.

Also, the hiring manager needs to help, as they often have an even better network than HR.

When the candidates come in for an interview, have a standardized scheme ready to assess their skills. The higher up, the more elaborate. It should consist of

- Presenting your vision of the company—does he/she share your vision of the future?

- Talk about examples from the past to check the above qualities (5 for leaders, 3 for team members)

- Have one or two real-life manual processes ready and ask them to make a proposal for automation

- Check for some logical and emotional intelligence

- Particularly for leaders: get three opinions other than yours (HR, top management, and peer)

After hiring successfully, this process is self-reinforcing. As soon as you have a significant group of right hires, they will be able to provide their network to help.

Reconsider your pay range

A new skill set might have a different pay—quite likely a higher one; this is inevitable. In order to avoid crazy decisions on individual hires, you need to define an adequate pay range for new skill sets. This pay range can also serve as an incentive for existing staff to change their ways, as it becomes an attractive reward for following up on the transition.

Finally,

you need to invest in your employer branding

This can happen on many levels. Start with little things like renaming openings into something more attractive.
For example, you should recruit a 'Business Analyst' rather than an 'Employee Reporting'.

Be present in universities and offer attractive internships and thesis topics. This needs to be covered by the hiring managers, not by HR. It is much more authentic for students if they meet their potential boss than a recruiter.

You can even consider renaming entire teams and organizations within your company to make a difference.

As a bottom line, the competition for talents gets tougher, more expensive, and requires more internal resources and attention. If it doesn't, you're not doing it right.

This investment, however, is sure to pay off.

Change for Existing Leaders

Already, in the chapter on Digital Operation Leaders, there has been some reflection on potential reactions and groups within your leadership team.

It is only being honest to say that not everyone from the existing leadership team will have or will develop the skills required to automate operations; some will even actively oppose it.

Still, there is a chance to make most—or in some cases, even all—of them join you in the transition.

The starting point is showing them the necessity of a digital change

You can use some of the reasoning here about the general trend toward digitalization, the potential in attracting new talent, and of course you can always present each one a copy of this book (something which would also be greatly appreciated by my editor!)

However, in order to be authentic and convincing, you will need to customize the reasoning to your particular situation.

If you manage to create an atmosphere of trust and honesty, each person will be able to tell you things in their daily work that are frustratingly slow, outdated or old-fashioned.

Take this as a starting point, reflect during long one-on-ones what their strategies are for overcoming these frustrations.

You will probably find them helpless at solving the challenges, or complaining about something bigger like: 'there is no management interest in my problem'.
Also, they often notice that the world around them has changed pace, and they notice the increasing gap between their reality and the digitalizing world, which makes them feel uncomfortable.

Your best bet is to

offer a solution and plan how to get digital

This will prove to be new and promising. At the same time, you will provide clear steps which make the topic much less scary than the vague threat they had sensed before.

Refer to established models of change management like the seven phases of change. Reflect on these with your leaders, so that you not only know where they stand (or got stuck) but also so that they know.

Managing to convince them of the necessity already represents phase 4 (Acceptance) in the seven-phase model. Allow time for 1-3 (Shock, Denial and Self Doubt) and don't forget to support 5-7 (Experimentation, Search for Meaning, and Integration).

Apart from the question of what needs to be done, one important issue remains:

Do your leaders have the necessary skills for the transition?

There probably will be a gap. It will help them a great deal if you really spell this out to them. What exactly is required?

What is already there? What needs freshening up, and what needs to be developed?

Turn this from the notion of being 'too old for this' into the notion of 'these are the 3 things you need to learn/improve on.' It gives them a fair chance, and at the same time may even be exciting for your leaders.

It will increase their capabilities, their skills, give them a guide into an exciting world, and increase their value in the job market.

It is crucial to be open and honest when identifying the skills required and the gaps

Even though the list of shortfalls might be big, it is important to make it complete. If it is not the full picture, there is no point in closing the gaps because they will simply not be sufficient.

This frankness will impose a certain amount of stress on your leaders, but it is called leaving your comfort zone because it is less comfortable—at least, at the start. Leaving the comfort zone is what needs to be done if change is to take place.

If you find leaders on your team who can bridge this gap and follow you on your transition, everything is fine.

Things become more difficult if there is no way to bring their abilities to the level at which you need them. When looking at the importance of your leadership team with

- translating this process into the team
- the abilities to communicate with IT
- the right focus on recruiting on a personal level
- the definition of the roadmaps and so on.

it is more than obvious that you will fail if you leave the wrong people in positions of responsibility.

Make a plan for how to replace them with the right people. Your first thought is probably about the question of what to do with the current leader. But the much more important one is: where do you find a new one?

Changing the department lead in the middle of a transition process adds stress, but having to replace a wrong hire, and thus creating a second change bears the potential for chaos. Focus on avoiding this and choose carefully.

Finding a solution for the old department lead is always an individual case and depends on many factors. His/her age, potential work alternatives, life situation, attitude (aggressive or co-operative), and so on.
One area which could add value, maybe, to help holding up the status quo until change kicks in. This requires the right attitude though.

It is also true that there can be constellations in which you need to continue without him/her.

This is never an easy decision; however, avoiding it is not an option. If you do, you will end up with the wrong people in the wrong positions and a significant group of (former) leaders nagging and opposing the change you have started.

This would not only be confusing for your team but also provide room for a mutiny of the past.

Turning it around, your task of making an old-fashioned operation digital is so much easier if you have the full support of your leaders.

Change on the Team Level

Some of the steps taken when introducing a digital transformation at the employee level are very similar to the ones on the leadership level.

Here, too, you need to explain the necessity, offer a plan for what needs to be done, identify required skills, and work on the gaps between those and current abilities.

However, there are also exist significant differences. The most important one is that

some areas of the daily work will remain almost unchanged for a long time. These have to continue functioning

Take pilots as an example. Even though technology allows for fully autonomous flights, it is likely that it will take a long time until regulations will allow for this.

At this time, there is little fundamental change in the job profile of a pilot. On the contrary, if you are an airline, you need pilots to keep up on operations.

In other areas, change is more pressing, and solutions are closer at hand. In these teams, you need to be clearer on what to expect and what needs to be done.

Sticking with the airline example, the check-in has changed from a fully manual process to a self-serve solution for most airlines.
Here, you now need people to optimize and supervise the

online check-in options, the self-serve terminals, and the luggage drop-offs.

Balancing Efficiency Gains and Job Security
Options for Avoiding Digitalization—None

Whenever manual processes are being automated, there is the immediate question of what will happen to the people who had been executing the process before?

There might even be a reflex not to do it, in order to 'protect' these jobs. But the truth is that

avoiding digitalization is costing more jobs than leading it

It is a simple exercise to understand every efficiency gain that is possible, but which you avoided in your company as a competitive disadvantage that could shrink your business or even sink it.

Unless you are operating in a monopoly or in public ownership, this is not an option.
And even in these cases, there comes a time at which your monopoly is challenged from the outside, or the public owner is fed up with a loss-making service.

Take the taxi monopoly in many countries as an example. In many places, the total number of taxis as well as tariffs are centrally decided, leaving the market with no competition on offer or price. The result was a very old-fashioned business that was and is still vulnerable to digital intruders like Uber or Lyft.

On the other hand, simply stating the economical necessity is not going to help anyone in your company who wants to know how their future looks.

This question needs to be addressed and answered clearly and openly. Anything else would be neither fair for the employees nor helpful for the company, because there would be no commitment or energy from the team to drive the change that is essential for success.

There are several strategies for managing this too. Some of them will be shown here, but they represent a general toolset.

You have to customize this process for your business and industry, and no two solutions will be completely identical. Keep in mind that

avoiding the topic of job security will inhibit your digitalization

Allow adequate time for elaborating on a strategy here.

Automation and digitalization don't come in the form of a big bang. They come as part of a culture.

Out of your dozens and hundreds of processes, you will only change a few at any given time. When doing so, you will work with prototypes, pilots, roll-out times, A-B tests, and so on. All of this will increasingly improve your efficiency.

Consider, as a rule of thumb, that if you end up with

1–2% efficiency gain per month –that is already a good rate

As a measure of efficiency, divide the cost of operations by the relevant turnover.

As a result, you are usually not looking for strategies to find new tasks for the bulk of your team, but for 1–2% per month.

I am aware that this is a little academic, but the point is that you're managing the question of getting the right people on the right job, and that is a totally different issue from laying off great teams.

Option 1: Natural churn in companies is between 1%–5% per month

depending on countries, industries, education levels, and so on.

However, even the most stable workforces in public services have around 10–15% churn per year. Using this natural fluctuation smartly should be part of your toolset.

Option 2: Growth rates help you

If you have a fast-growing business, your efficiency is growing already if you don't hire as turnover increases. Combining this with the natural churn mentioned above usually puts you in a position where, even if you do hire prudently, your efficiency rises. The few hires you make should fit your digital roadmap.

Option 3: Training new skills to motivated people

There will be a lot of people on your team with great ideas and the drive to change things. Give them the training they need to develop this energy into skills.

This could be training on agile management or applying tools that will become new industry standards. It could also be things like English classes, as it is the leading language for the digital world.

People willing to improve their skills will benefit their personal careers, bring enthusiasm into teams, and allow you to manage the required skills better, as you can select the areas you need.

With these tools at hand, one important exercise is still missing. Alongside explaining the need and strategy for digitalization,

you have to honestly break down the effects on the teams for at least 12 months into the future

Once your teams learn to trust this outlook—and you need to stick to the promise, of course—they will know what will happen in which team.

You can and should help them move into the right direction. It will ease the transition if the same people who are supposed to hold up the old process, until it is replaced, know what their personal future will be afterwards.

Limitations of Managing the Desire for Job Security

Regardless of the efforts you make, there will be people in your team who will demand full stability in their routines, and who will refuse and ignore all the help provided to adjust their ways.

On a personal level, this is sometimes understandable, but it ignores the changing times. If people stubbornly refuse to join in a transition, there is eventually no other way to continue than without them.

When managing this, it is important to make it crystal clear in your internal communication that it is the behavior of the individual (or even the group) that makes such a decision necessary.

For a lack of attitude, there is no outside solution

Their desire for job security is understandable, but their expectation of an eternally unchanging work environment is simply unrealistic.

New Technology Attracting a New Workforce

Let me close this sensitive chapter, and at the same time this book, with a promising outlook.

As you may recall from the introduction, there is a significant gap between people working in classic tech environments and people working in old-school operations.

If you are determined to transform your operations into a digital work mode, you can bridge this gap by applying the various methods described in this book.

The result is a different attitude at all levels. People working in your operations will be proud to do so. Colleagues from other departments will notice that operations is no longer the unfathomable slow burden of the company, but a driver of change and innovation.

On the job market, word will spread that this is the place to be for achieving great things.

You will have overcome the prestige deficit of operations, at least, for your business. This will lead to an upward spiral.

Talents from outside of the company will want to be part of this. The barrier to changing jobs between, for example, IT and operations will dissolve. And as it is possible to change in and out of operations, career paths are no longer one-way streets, leading into operations but never out again.

This will inspire operations, as well as other teams, all the way up to management. It will be taken seriously—perhaps even as a benchmark.

This new quality in the team skills of operations will eventually lead to a leap in your product quality, due to the reliable, automated processes in efficiency on the cost side, and constant innovation.

It is this spirit that made the classic digital applications so fruitful, and you will have successfully introduced them into business.

AFTERWORD BY FLIXBUS CO-FOUNDER DANIEL KRAUSS

What do people think when they think of FlixBus or what is presently FlixMobility? Even now, Flix is being used as a synonym for long distance bus travelling in Europe. On the one hand, this makes us extremely proud, but on the other, this does not exactly tell the truth about what Flix really is and why it is so special and has eventually been successful over the last 7 years.

FlixMobility is actually both or even more than a bus company; it is a long-distance ground transportation mobility provider; some call it a platform. As complicated as this term seems, it just as easily shows what kind of company you can find under the surface. What the company does in a nutshell is take care of a superior, software-driven platform which brings supply and demand together smartly, and at the same time, takes the responsibility of over 350 mobility partners to safely drive our customers from their point of origin to their destination.

So, can it be said that FlixMobility is an Uber for buses then? Not really. In comparison to plain vanilla platforms emerging out of the Silicon Valley, Flix has built a vertically integrated platform that combines the advantages of both worlds, fast growth and flexibility as well as tackling barriers for swift entry into the market. Therefore, operations at Flix is at the forefront of closing the gap between the tech world and the normal world, which has over time become much more important than was originally intended.

Managing a global business entails its own complexities. In the case of mobility, it is not the platform that needs to be managed; rather, the discussion is focused on currencies and taxes. It concerns the high number of passengers and vehicles being managed. In this arena, solutions to operations makes the difference. Flix reached this point last, but then, it invested and created meaningful solutions (watch dogs) to control a worldwide fleet.

As you have read before, operations has to overcome one stigma: it leads to a loss of prestige because operations is merely a subject in management if it fails. This is certainly true, but at the same time, it is something that operations organizations have had to deal with always, which actually makes them quite similar to tech organizations where the same stigma has been present since forever.

In this area, the burden with legacy systems truly comes into play, since their durability and reliability is getting lower over time. Also, their taxes are increasing. Tech tax is something which always has to be considered when bringing an organization to the age of digitization. Each system comes with taxes, the cost you have to dedicate and continuously pay for running it. Basically, age is the basis on which tech-tax is applied to, like salary in real life. It is almost never less than 20%. So, tech companies need to stay young within their systems in order to avoid tax.

Why is this that important? At least for Flix, it is crucial because we want to at least somehow predict the future of mobility in order to be able to co-shape it. To achieve that, both a super modern tech as well as a flawlessly running operations are crucial. Well, modern is not in itself that meaningful, it has to come with the ability to always be able to adapt quickly, in particular, to customer needs. Customer who experienced changes in both the software and the bus product determined Flix's success. It is important to understand that a software alone cannot be modular and agile before the company does not achieve that first: Conway's law would be an interesting follow-up reading to understand this. Therefore, cross-functional independent organizational units are the success goals. And independent does not mean operations being independent from its tech, but operations including its tech being independent from marketing, not to mention both have to simultaneously focus on the customer and therefore the sustainable success of the company.

So far, Flix has been able to manage this also; but this has neither given it the freedom to be complacent nor the guarantee of future success. One must remember that the only bad thing about success is that it always reflects the past, not the future. Exactly because of this, FlixMobility is not just lucky to be a child of digitalization, it makes considerable effort to stay agile and not lose this advantage. Or, as Jeff Bezos said, always stay at the day 1 level. This takes a lot of focus, the will to succeed and to be competitive and win each and every customer every day of every year. In order to retain that kind of appetite, a great willingness to continuously change and learn is mandatory as well as staying flexible as humans and an organization. This mindset precisely will not only ensure FlixMobility remains successful, but it also makes the best job guarantee in the age of digitization.